Late Autumn Sunlight

Late Autumn Sunlight

East Anglian Verses

by

Martin Newell

Linocuts by James Dodds

Jardine Press Ltd

2007

First published by
Jardine Press in 2001

Extended Second Edition
Jardine Press Ltd 2007
www.jardinepress.co.uk

Copyright © Martin Newell
Linocuts copyright © James Dodds
Edited by Elly Robinson

ISBN 978-0-9552035-4-1

Contents

Introduction

An introduction, in fact, to a pair of
collaborationists who need no introduction.
There cannot be many parts of Britain where
a local scene is so well caught by poet and
artist together. Were it not for Martin Newell
and James Dodds today's East Anglia, and
especially coastal North-East Essex, would, like
so many places, be identified in the usual
generalised terms of a commuting area, plus
some inviting tourist language. But they will
have none of this and between them they have
for a long time now revealed the true nature
of their homeland. Martin Newell casts a
protective eye over it. There is nothing he
cannot see and nothing he cannot value.
Although his vision is proprietorial, he wants to
share it. He has a genius for relating the past
to the present and not making all kinds of
things sound out-dated. His poetry is an inven-
tory of the region. He does not deal in "by-
gones" but in what connects. He is affectionate-
ly caustic, witty and moving, a great local voice
which, via a stream of work in *The Independent*,
is listened to far and wide. He has always pos-
sessed a sad ear for decline, for the running-
down but not the vanishing of things, and *Late
Autumn Sunlight* is a subject which suits him. It
is wry, funny, profound, a signpost to what
could so easily be missed, wonderful sights,
unique detail, views which change the reader's
perspective. Which is what poetry is for.

Martin Newell could not have found a better
sharer of his vision than James Dodds. His

strong linocuts provide a perfect accompani-
ment to the words but rightly do not attempt
to illustrate them. Where the poet lists the real
natives, the real activities of his corner of the
world, the artist takes its harbours back to
their essentials of shipping, storytelling,
worship and domesticity. The populations of
Aldeburgh and Wivenhoe are captured –
walled-up, almost – between soil and sea.
James Dodds also captures that freedom of the
coast which makes sailors and fishermen
another race. Both he and Martin Newell have
a wary delight in local legends and *Late Autumn
Sunlight* contains an extract from *Black Shuck*,
to my mind a masterly re-telling of Eastern
England's ghostly dog tale. Shuck makes the
Hound of the Baskervilles sound like man's
best friend. The Newell version, with Dodds'
pictures, is classic folklore and not to be
missed.

Martin Newell's East Anglia tumbles about
untidily, and points a finger at contemporary
suburban standards. "Where is your soul?" he
consistently asks. It is a question we have to
answer. Is it in theme parks, in the tarted-up
pub, at the rat-race? James Dodds' East Anglia
is crafted in shipyards, farmyards and work-
shops, including the studios of its many artists.
These were for him during his youth the places
where skill came from hands, not words. A
shipwright tells his apprentice, "I shan't say
noth'n. *You* watch *me*" Newell and Dodds show
how close they are in this first poem of their
latest book. Their work is a combination of
doing – and dreaming. Its pace is set to some

extent by the poet's bike and by the slowed-up discipline of the linocut. Nothing flashes past them or is dashed off. There is contemplation. East Anglians are returned to their roots, non-natives given a delightful crash course on what these coastal counties really are, on what made them.

Frequently local writers and artists go over the old ground, the famous names and villages, the much repeated customs and the tourist routes. But not here. Martin Newell "sings" what both East Anglia and its visitors would never see. Modest lanes, ordinary people, not "characters", the minutiae of life, marvellously personal sightings of birds and plants are brought to our attention. He is a poet who says, "Look at what you are missing!" James Dodds' work is an act of love which incorporates a sturdy reality and legend. His small coastal towns are anchorages for other things as well as ships. Martin Newell has more to say about the latest inhabitants than the oldest inhabitants, and caustically. He sees East Anglia under constant invasion by one horde or another but able to hold its own. Humanity and its detritus ultimately touches his heart. So here is a two-man guide to the edges of Norfolk, Suffolk and particularly to border-line Essex; some poems and pictures which will make us look at them differently.

Ronald Blythe.
2001

Anthem For Essex

Tilty, Wimbish, Stebbing, Shopland
Chipping Ongar, Ingatestone
All the market towns and hamlets
On the rivers Crouch or Colne
West of Walton, east of Easton
Shellow Bowells to Hanningfield
London's bread-bin, lungs and love-nest
Beaches, birdland, wood and weald
Essex. Seaxes, sheaves and shield.

Here the horsemen met for racing
Here the highwaymen were hung
Here the painter saw the skyline
Here the tide would poke its tongue
In among the samphire saltings
While the sun set sea alight
Here the smugglers moved the malmsey
Up the creek in dead of night
Customs cutter out of sight.

Saucy, sexy, seaside Essex
Driest place in British Isles
Where the robbers took retirement
When the Sweeney shut the files
Home of rock and naughty rhythms
Pirates, Paramounts and Procul
Harum, Hotrods, Ian Dury
Dr Feelgood – they were local
With Lee Brilleaux on lead vocal.

Epic Essex, best for bike-rides
Liberally laced with lanes
Pubs to punctuate the pedalling
Flower-baskets hung on chains
Coastal Essex – secret rivers
Heron-haunted waterland
Where the silver light in autumn
Lingers for a saraband
On the shingle and the sand.

Here are tales of long-dead writers,
Ghostly bikers, missing planes
Council gardens, scrapyards, thatches
Cricket matches seen from trains
Yellow fields in dazzled springtime
Varnished by a Van Gogh sky
Blind the copses and the spinneys
Where the rooks are building high
And the world goes skating by

Where the weatherboarded cottage
Waits in moddy monochrome
Nestling with new commuters
And the future coming home
Envious London, stuck in traffic
Simmering its quiet desires
Senses Essex spanning endless
Hazier than orchard fires
Out beyond those distant spires.

Excerpt from **Shipshape**

In this old shed and that old shed
The sound of saw and adze was wed
To mallet, hammer, chisel, file
And sanding, sanding all the while.
Old boys who knew these waters here
Worked hard, spoke little, drank their beer
Knew every inlet, creek and quay
From Burnham up to Brightlingsea
Told Jamie, shipwright yet-to-be
"I shan't say noth'n. You watch me"
No more than that and graft concerned
Since this is how the craft was learned
In bits and bats and splintered wood
Until at last the boy made good.

In salt-marsh, towpath, shingle, mud
The Essex coast gets in the blood
In sea-kale, samphire, gorse and sedge
Which grows along the water's edge
Till further in, the wetland yields
To hazy summer mangold fields
The copses, hedgerows, tractor-tracks
With pallets of potato sacks
And houses hidden in the lanes
With Flemish roofs and weathervanes
The churches closed, or overgrown,
The flowers left in grass unmown
Except around a tended tomb
From long-lived bride to long-dead groom.

And here a heron, there a lark
A curlew calling in the dark
To break the silence in the night
When moonlight drapes the boatyard white
And as the tides drain back to sea
From many-channelled estuary
Exposing ribs, remains of ships
The mud devours, it smacks its lips
Till deeper down and all around
The estuary's digestive sound
On windless nights pervades the air
When nothing stirs the maidenhair
And marker buoys stare up and blink
To see the stars return their wink.

The tide bleeds out and in the mud
The ships squat down, deprived of blood
Their buxom hulls exposed to air
The shipwright's exhibition there
Is free of charge and on display
The whole year round and twice a day
The curves, the clinker boards and keel
– The parts the water helped conceal –
Are testimony to an art
Much older craftsmen helped impart
In whispers down the estuary
I shan't say noth'n. You watch me.
Until it reached the river beds
From these old sheds and those old sheds.

Excerpt from **Shipshape Underway**

Out from Colchester, southwest
The countryside was unimpressed
When city gossip reached its ears
It stayed unchanged and slept for years
In weatherboarded modest gown
Where hamlet turned to tiny town
And elm-lined lanes lay in between
And railway trains had never been.

For instance, why should Totham care
What London said or did down there?
The crop came in, the barn was full
The haywain high, a horse to pull
The cart to town and fetch it back
Saw parson stopped along the track
To gaze across the great flat fields
And calculate his master's yields
In buried, married, newly-born
His sea, the waving Essex corn.

In north-east Essex, in the spring
The schedule doesn't mean a thing
At least not to the stubborn wind
By which the season's underpinned
The sun is strong, the blackthorn snows
The dirty evening darkness goes
But still the east wind slices throats
Mocking scarves and cutting coats
Pinching, clenching, killjoy crone
Tacking inland up the Colne
Flinging insults at the sun
Ruining the tourists' fun
And if she comes on Easter Day
She'll often linger most of May

But stuff like this breeds stubborn sons
Across the marsh the sound of guns
At practice with the halliards' rattle
Mingles with the mooing cattle
Turned out on the slopes for spring
Now the larks and thrushes sing
Then the gulls and waders call
Poet and artiist know them all
Noting them while working on
To see another winter gone.

19

River to River

The River Colne meanders slow
Through fecund farmlands, rainy green
A ribbon strewn across the floor
Of shallow valleys, hardly seen
Or guessed at from the Essex shore

East to Colchester and on
Its ullages and spillages
The houses and their secrets tucked
In hamlets and the villages
Around the Chappel viaduct

To Fordstreet, Fordham Bridge it goes
And idles by the Essex Way
Strengthened by St Botolph's Brook
It sidles by the road to pay
Its namesake Roman town a look

Widening there, it picks up speed
Skirting fields towards the mill
Where it stopped to pay a tithe
Beside the bridge below the hill
Before it hurried to The Hythe

Haggling with the tide for business
When the ships sailed up the Colne
Galleys, luggers, barges, smacks
Buildings plonked like Toblerone
Where they once unloaded sacks

Now the new estates are fronting
Toytown wharfs that dwarf the marshes
Wivenhoe and Brightlingsea
Wearing them like false moustaches
Edging up the estuary

Here the Saxon Sea comes hacking
While the River Colne expands
Mersea Flats and Cocum Hills
Gazing south to Maplin Sands
Where the biggest river spills

Now the blood of other rivers:
Crouch, Blackwater, Medway, Swale
Mingle, eddy, dash the shoreline
As container cargoes sail
Round the Thames's yawning jawline.

Shimmying up that serpent river
Go the humble and the great
– Other rivers' sons and daughters,
While the bouncers on the gate:
Kent and Essex, watch the waters

Coalhouse Point to Richmond Lock
Galleon's Reach to Watney's Brewery
Flotsam, jetsam, oil and beer
Hogarth sits with Ian Dury
Dreaming Cherry Garden Pier

Underneath that dirty duvet
Of the sky, the river swells
Carrying simple craft to fame
In a carillon of bells
Drowning others in its shame

Carrying sons of Colne to London
With a daubing or a ditty
To the busy landing stages
And the currents of the city
As it has throughout the ages.

Excerpt from **Black Shuck** –
The ghost dog of Eastern England

The moon across the marshes
The lonely Essex Marshes
Through rotting bones of barges in the mud
The east wind calls the curlew
Who pipes his cry the same
As when the rivers ran with Saxon blood

Where Byrhtnoth, earl of Essex
A thousand years before
Lost Maldon to the seawolves, Olaf's Danes
And fell among the dying
The horses of his ceorls
Ran riderless, no hands to hold the reins

And Northey Island's slaughter
Was carried by the wind
To Tiptree, Totham, Tollesbury and beyond
When Essex was the frontline
And Saxons clashed with Danes
For forest, field, hanger, creek and pond

And then along the causeway
Did Shuck come slinking out
To snuffle round the bodies of the dead?
Their shattered swords and shields
Their corslets oozing gore
And only ravens circling overhead

For from these misty marshes
These sucking, popping marshes
The Dog jumps up and soundlessly goes by
To parish, copse and crossroad
Through churchyard, lane and field
Then you, or someone close to you may die.

Thorpe Market

The bric-a-brac and gaudy tack
Of any generation
Are sold for pennies not for pounds
At Thorpe-le-Soken station
And kept in circulation

The portrait of King Edward swings
In creaking celebration
And peels by the public house
At Thorpe-le-Soken station
In which they serve libation

Then plant and flower auctions
In rusting iron sheds
Are filled with Essex faces
On weathered turnip heads
From Clacton or from Toosy
With their end of winter colds
Who bid at Thorpe-le-Soken
For a box of marigolds
At one pound-eighty? Eighty-five?
Ninety, do I hear?
They stick at one pound-ninety
And sod the auctioneer
Who glances over half-moon specs
With keen and practised eye
At hardy annual gardeners
Who won't be hoist so high

And paperbacks laid up in stacks
Defying your concentration
Are found on trestles ten-a-pound
At Thorpe-le-Soken station
Some still in publication

The prices paid for literature
Immune here to inflation
Where Barbara Cartland lies with Joyce
At Thorpe-le-Soken station
For your imagination

But despite the April sunshine
There's an easterly which wields
A cutting edge to chill you
From the Thorpe-le-Soken fields
And there beneath the conker tree
In quiet resignation
The traders turn their collars up
At Thorpe-le-Soken station
And curse their occupation

The maltings by the railyard
The legend says it plain
Make malt for Double Diamond
You'll read it from the train
You can smell it in the market
You can taste it in the rain
And it lingers in your nostrils
Till you're nearly home again

Then market women's wartime eyes
Are closed in concentration
To tally takings in the pub
By Thorpe-le-Soken station
A tricky operation

And I may have a drink or two
Of devil's embrocation
I like to watch the trains go by
At Thorpe-le-Soken station
And miss my destination.

The Corner Shop

Barton Stores as run by Pat and Gordon
Beside the railway bridge, a corner shop
Sold matches, household soap and coal
Bin bags, candles, kitchen roll
The things without which normal life might stop

And after clocks went back in late October,
In tea-time traffic of the afternoon
A scent of ripened Cox's
Met flames from burning boxes
And rose to reach a pale grapefruit moon

Halfway down the High Street, summer mornings
Pat's dulcet voice would ring to rout the birds
Her old pronunciation
Quaint to a population
Already drowned in Estuary words

But lemons, pomegranates, limes
And Spanish chestnuts, clementines
Egyptian spuds, African grapes
From stony hills and sunny capes
Whose violet skies and white-flecked shores
Were worlds away from Barton Stores
Could bring a taste, a scent, a spray
Of summer on a winter's day

Then on a blustery Sunday in the springtime
The shop filled up with weekend roasting smells
While sailors headed seawards
And drinkers ambled quay-wards
In cherry blossom snow and churchyard bells

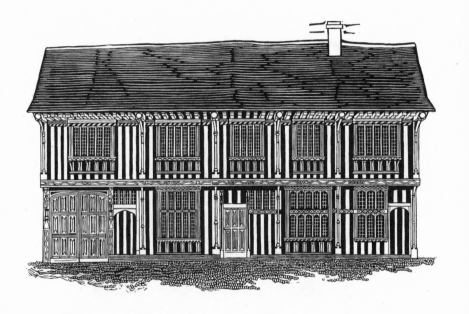

So ended half a century – and an era
The rueful moments of the closing day
And as the shop quit trading
A ghost pulled down the shading
And watched a chunk of England fall away.

The North Sea

This is the sea the sailor saw
Which thrashed the shingle on the shore
Swallowed sloops and galleons whole
Yet gave up herrings by the shoal
The 'silver treasure' called by men
Built Blythburgh – a fish church then
Paid for its windows and chimeres
Though took back Dunwich in arrears

This is the sea of winter geese
Its gun-grey, bird-limed, heaving fleece
The Whale Road where the Saxons went
To settle Suffolk, Essex, Kent.
Cold currents fetched the codfish down
Filled ketches, smacks and fed the town
And sped the skillingers to bring
The oysters back from Terschelling

This was a sea of working ways
Of dirty, bleach-stained denim days
Where little ships from net-strewn quays
Their halliards rattling in the breeze
Set out with men in set-jawed mood
To turn their labours into food
Who knew, when fishing quotas bit
That nothing good could come of it

This was a sea of fish and birds
And all the figures, facts and words
On how its creatures disappear
Cannot convey its troubles here
Nor any pious why-oh-whying.
The sea, the old North Sea is dying
And muffles in its warming swell
The tolling of the Dunwich bell.

Warriors –

on finding the body of a Saxon chief and his horse
at a Suffolk airbase

A Saxon chieftain and his horse
Lay undisturbed in chalky ground
For fourteen hundred years or so
And slept the centuries away.

Much later, over farms and fens
Around a Suffolk air-force base
A younger German warrior flew
But fell to earth and lost the day.

"Well met", the Saxon soldier said
"We've changed a bit since oxen carts
Though not so fast you'd notice it
They take their time around these parts.

Where warriors younger now than you
Still gird themselves for battle zones
Lie down young flier, the day will come
When men will marvel at your bones."

To a Postmistress Upon Retiring

The march of time went past the place
Its staples, pens and paperclips
Dockets, forms in duplicate
Postal orders, stamps and glue
Aged twenty-six, she took the shop
Way back in nineteen forty-two
When land girls were her customers.
The airmen, soldiers, farming men
And chaps with different accents
Sent letters home to lonely wives
As warplanes raked the Norfolk skies

In 'forty-five, the boys came home
'Forty-seven, froze for weeks
Starving birds tapped window panes
And rationing was still in place

Through the dreary flooded fifties
Headscarved women, men in caps
Blazing skiffle summers, bees,
Telegrams on motor bikes
Whitsun weekend, 'sixty-four,
On scooter run to Sheringham,
A lost patrol of London mods
Who puttered slowly past her door

In all that time and all those years
Of Christmas cards and sisal string
She'd license dogs and wirelesses
Motor cars and TV sets
Her weighing scales, arithmetic
And common sense were all she had

Then half a century on or so
Up comes bold Efficiency
Who won't leave well enough alone
And says she must be 'putered-up
Hard-disk, screen and god-knows-what
Can't be doing with all that.
Pen and paper did the lot
"Wun't be druv." She shut the shop.

*"Wunt be druv" in the last line, is old Norfolk dialect
for: "won't be driven."*

The New Rural Vision

As I strode out one evening
In stockman's coat and hat
Genuine. Obtained from magazine.
I saw a host of houses
In yonder far-off fields
A place no longer designated green

The ranks of parked Hyundais
Gleamed bright on cobbled drives
With paintwork which no mud had ever splashed
In spears of fractured lamplight
From Pullman-curtained rooms
Where Tweedy met with Twee and quietly clashed

The claggy, rutted farm-tracks
Were strewn with bark and chip
Directions arrowed blue on wooden posts
While in the middle-distance
A phalanx of kagouls
Advanced upon the weekend-homes of hosts

A re-skilled border collie
Stood counselling the sheep
Assistance now the term, not Rounding Up
Liaising with Team Leader,
A "motivated" ram
Who formerly had held the job of Tup

A cockerel with a contract
Laid out in simple terms
Restricting crowing hours from ten 'til four
Perched sullen on a hen house
A bandage on his beak
And scanned the thing for any legal flaw

34

And as I wandered further
I chanced upon some trees
Now clearly marked an Ancient Woodland Site
I hadn't really nailed them
As anything but Woods
Though had they not been signposted, I might

And everywhere were warnings
To farmers and their kin
Forbidding muddy tractors on the road
"Please bag and bin your cowdung
And keep your sheep on leads."
New Labour says:
Respect The Country Code.

The Cycle Path

On a bicycle in winter
Back to Wivenhoe alone
When the smoky Rowhedge rooftops
Through the mist across the Colne
Are forgotten Saxon farmsteads
And the cattle stand like stone
On a still day in December
At the turning of the tide
With the fading roar of traffic
As the Hythe is left behind
For the patterned frosty woodland
Where the leaf-veins in the mud
Are the skeletons of fairies
Delicately strewn around
Then the only living sound
Is the wingbeat of a swan
As it flaps its way upriver
Past the moorhens in the sedge
To a white armada waiting
Silent at the water's edge.

On a bicycle in summer
In the horny pagan heat
Racing with a pleasure steamer
Where the rail and river meet
As a woman on the sun-deck
Sees the cyclist on the path
And she smiles, waving madly
Till he disappears in trees
Where the splinters of the sunlight
Splash the hawthorn leaves with gold
And the hollow-way is dappled
Where the burning ball has rolled
When the winter lost a wicket
After spring came in and bowled
A bluebell haze, the smell of rain
The thunder of the London train
A ship's wash jostles driftwood high
The seagulls see the bikes go by
And shriek along the estuary
To Brightlingsea. To Brightlingsea.

Thorrington Tide Mill

Treading on pedals up Tenpenny Hill
The Brightlingsea buses may find you
Racing the sunset to Thorrington Mill
Only the wind to remind you
The best of the weather's behind you

Tenpenny Brook goes trickling down
Shimmying over the gravel and sand
Turning the tilth of the centuries softly
Sifting the soil with a quicksilver hand

Thorrington Mill sat chugging and churning
Digging a living from out of the mud
Pushing the paddles that milled for the Normans
Scooping the tide which provided her blood

Groaning a protest from deep in her belly
Over the farmland, the barking of dogs
Wallower rolling and chattering damsel
Grinding their teeth went the old wooden cogs

Times when the stonedressers came to the marshes
Sallied from Colchester up to the mill
Journeyman, Master, Apprentice and *Boy*
Cut into millstone with thrift and its bill

Late after Lammas, with geese in the stubble
Picking the carcass of harvest-time bare
Fruit-weighted hedgerows and summer in trouble
Miller still working and damp in the air

Slackwater days when the mudflats go silver
Late, like a lord deep in debt, comes the sun
Peering past trees in the haze of September
Dusty old windows of Thorrington Mill
Waiting for wagons from Tenpenny Hill.

The Ruins of St. Peter's Church

The ruins of St. Peter's Church
Sleep on and twice a month or so
From March until October goes,
An unseen gardener comes to mow
Trims the yews and strims the weeds
And now removes the perished wreaths
Their twisted leaves and rusted wire
To pile upon an autumn pyre
In some quiet corner, well away
From any business of the day

Roofless, open to the sky
The ruins yawn, the clouds go by
The crows and rooks and rabbits pass
Across the floor long-laid to grass.
While ivy on the chancel flowers
On porous Roman brick and lime
The medieval mortar sours
In walls that crumble over time
And overshadow broken crypts
Where winter drags its fingertips

And in the churchyard, overgrown
The women mostly come alone
Bring cloth and brush to clean the stone
Chrysanthemums to deck the urns
Scissors, secateurs and twine
As melancholy at their tasks
They battle briony and bine
On solitary afternoons
Lose themselves in memories
Of husbands, homes, and harvest moons

Then, once a week, along the track
A cyclist rattles, looking back
Across the furrowed centuries
At quiet familiar things he sees
A ghost parade of country folk
The long-dead farmers and their wives
The spirits in the wayside oak
Where thistledown goes drifting south
Through ruins of St. Peter's Church
Towards the silver river mouth.

The Shipyard

Bramble, Southernwood and Dock
Unsung among the rubble
Were the salvagemen and saviours
Of a shipyard long in trouble:

"Mr. Bramble," said his colleague
"Since these premises are ours,
Will you formally confirm it
In the trademark of your flowers?
Now the welders won't return here
And the riveters have gone
We must be about our business
As the summer's getting on."

"Mr. Southernwood, the matter
Of this concrete still remains
It may crack with your persistence
And I see you've made some gains
But we fight a losing battle
With the tyrant of the clock
May I venture you prevail upon
The strengths of Mr. Dock?"

"Mr. Dock, you've made some progress
Since removal of the cranes
If the rusty sun assists us
And the heavy summer rains
We could sign the final papers
And conclude this sorry case
Leaving Mr. Moon as watchman
When the winter's on the place."

The War Memorials of Norfolk

Muffled within vastnesses of Norfolk
The dusty cough of half-forgotten names
Remembered by old men in market taverns
Who stare in flames

From Southrepps, Blickling, Corpusty or Bacton
From Matlaske, Stratton Strawless, Alby Hill
They straggled like a badly-drilled militia
And then lay still

The conflict bawled its challenge out so loudly
That even these quiet places woke and heard
The exclamation marks became memorials
For war, the word

Weather-pitted now, they stand in churchyards
Or modest squares, behind grey posts and chain
The poppy wreaths in early winter sunlight
Turned pink by rain

And over time, beneath that scarecrow skyline
Across flat fields they drifted back alone
Ghosts who haunted grieving, sea-eyed sweethearts
Their names in stone.

The Last Ferry

When the chestnut slopes are rusty
And the Roman River still
And the reeds the only sentinels
From here to Chopping's Mill
Since the spirits of the legionaries
All returned to Rome,
With autumn in the saltings
You will take the ferry home

The last one of October
And the loneliest of the year
Past blackened ribs of barges
Where the only sound you hear
Is the bickering of seagulls
In a melancholy sky
And the coughing of the engine
At the season sculling by

Then the swans reclaim the jetty
As the ferry slips from sight
And the sun goes down with jaundice
In a burst of dirty light
Till the shimmer of the windows
From the houses on the hill
Sends a semaphore of sunset
To the crows at Chopping's Mill

And Anchor Hill lies dozing
In the smoke of Sunday fires
And the starlings sit like symphonies
Unplayed upon the wires
And the ferry skipper's silent
At the closing of the day
As the sun creeps out of Quay Street
And the boat is put away.

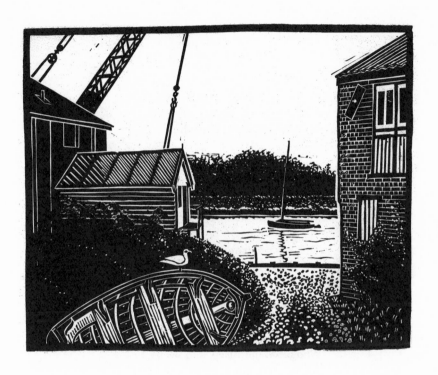

Modern Village Life

My bike-lights pry down shiny drives
When watery autumn evenings fall
Where faux-Victorian bollards stand
"Dunhagglin" Three hundred grand

Intruder lights snap on at night
To bathe the place in stalag white
The witch-hat gable, weathercock
And mock-colonial schoolhouse clock

The carriage wheels built into gate
For barn converted into home
With panoramic window view
And weatherboards a deal too new

That distant man who shut the bank
It's partly him you have to thank
For helping close the grocer's down
And drive their business out of town

Into the maws of superstores
Who bleed the village into sleep
You're going to need a car you know
A mudless four wheel? There you go

Essential for the darkened lanes
And best of all with bull-bars on
To guard against pedestrians
The cyclists and equestrians

Now driving will be half your life
The surgery, post office, pub
And to your station miles away
Then ride-on mower, on Saturday

Your kids can haunt the village green
To numb themselves on nasty beer
Then out of minds, get out of hand
Before they move to bedsit-land

No shadows to disquiet you here
But ghosts of yokels on the road
A most exclusive residence
From In-Like-Flynn Developments.

49

Severe Weather Warning

I gotta get along now
Thass time for me to goo
I woulda stayed on longer but . . .
I think thass goornta snoo

Thass got as far as Croomer
My auntie toold me soo
She telephooned especially . . .
I think thass goornta snoo

Me feet got coold this morn'n
And generally they do
Thass even if I'm workin' . . .
I think thass goornta snoo

The wind comes off Siberia
Then when it start to bloo
That tend to cut right through you . . .
I think thass goornta snoo

If that gets far as Aylsham
Then Norwich gets it too
And they'll knoo all about it . . .
I think thass goornta snoo

They got a foot last winter
That only goos to shoo
It happens to us moost years . . .
I think thass goornta snoo

I think thass goornta snoo
I doon't jest think – I knoo
Doon't say I never toold you . . .
I think thass goornta snoo
I do.

Frinton Rap

Twelve-inch Crinkletown Mix

Take a north EAST Essex TRAIN
Any wet DAY in the rain
And you change at THORPE for Kirby Cross
To a place where there's no CANDY floss
And you find yourself at FRINTON
Say wha?
I said FRINton
That's CRINKLETOWN where the old go to
To get aWAY from the likes of YOU
All the younger people LOOK bored
And dogs are BANNED from the GREENsward
And there are no PUBS
So no-one GOES
And they banned TRANSISTOR radios
Cos they've never heard of HIP hop
And there isn't any CHIP shop
And you can't CHANGE on the BEACH
And there's no BUS – so you're out of REACH
Of CLACton and WALton
If it's FRINton where you're coming from

Take a walk ROUND the AVENUES
Where there's blue RINSE in the PINK loos
And a Mathers-Platt   What is that?
It's a thief alarm on a GRANNY FLAT
There's a golf-club bar in CRINKLETOWN
But you can't get IN so you walk on DOWN
Past the BEACH huts and the WET rocks
And the crumbling wartime PILL-BOX
Which they built to keep the GERMANS out
And it must have worked – there are none about
So you stand THERE in the rain
It's a long wait till YOUR train
And you're cold BORED and thinking then
That the average age of a citizen
Must be N-n-n-n-Ninety. N-n-n-n-n Ninety
YO FRINTON

Talkin' Essex

They don't talk Essex here n'more
The jigsaw coast and Saxon shore
That framed the flatlands and its farms
Have fallen into London's arms
Scythed and stacked in stooks, the accent
Disappeared, the sounds moved on
Rabbits flushed from fields, forgotten
Now the good old boys have gone

"Alroight then, buoy? Yep, that'll dew."
Reckon? Yeahp! Moind how yer goo.
North ter Toozy, south to Leighs
What ever are you growen? Peas."
Good old boys who'd sat on settles
As their dads had done before
Stillage, flags and copper kettles
Spit and sawdust on the floor

Housing sprawled beside the barleys
East End Brendas, West End Charlies
Limehouse Lennies, Wapping dockers
Romford Teds, then mods and rockers,
Now? Their kids in souped-up motors
Daz and Shaz, the Eighties voters
Estuary Nation's birth:
"'Ere – Guess 'ow much my 'ouse is worf?"

"Or-wight, then? I'll tell you wot;
Get yer wedge aht. Mutchchoo got?
I'm 'Ank Marvin. Ahhjoo fiwl?
Less go'n'ave 'n Indian miwl
Uvver nigh' righ'? Daniella
Tiffany and and Shayne – 'er fella?
Drinkin' Aftershocks and Stella
Got frown aht this Bierkella."

In Autumn Attic

Autumn came to Wivenhoe and slowly
Turned to ash the opal of the sky
Lovers took the last train out of Clacton
Drunken insects zig-zagged home to die

Dutiful, the widow of the summer
Drifted through the apple-scented halls
This year's girl-most-likely-to was hanging
Rusty leaves on musty redbrick walls

Westerlies, the stagehands of the season
Moved to shift the scenery away
Ruffled up the river down to Rowhedge
Drew the evening in to close the day

Somewhere through the trees, a train to London
Sparked the overheads and slid from sight
Deeper in the woods a dog was barking
Someone on the station said goodnight

Huddled in the pub, the early drinkers
Turned to see the window spanked by rain
Not to hear the calling of the curlew
Nor the ghosts of children in the lane.

The Winter Bonfire

Professor Winsten loved a fire
He'd don thin coat and wander out:
"Anything that I can do?"
He'd ask me. I'd disguise my doubt
Fragile, in his seventies
Boyish in some other ways
I handed him hide-gloves, a rake
And watched him, while he fed the blaze

The bonfire, bright against the grey
Our custom in those old Decembers
Standing in encroaching darkness
Gazing into orange embers
From the cuttings, canes and deadwood
Apple, rose and artichoke
Came the wraiths of vanquished summer
Snaking out of sparks and smoke

Further off, the coughing lorries
Chucking out their mucky load
Mumbled at the grumbling buses
Squeezing into Station Road
While Professor Winsten's bonfire
Billowed through the afternoon
Till the final wisps of woodsmoke
Rose to meet the churchyard moon.

The Funeral of a Young Man

Wakes Colne White Colne
Earls Colne and Colne Engaine
Rainwashed green in early summer
As I cycle home again
Past the Chappel viaduct
Only memories will remain
Wakes Colne White Colne
Earls Colne and Colne Engaine

At the church – St. Peter's Halstead
Cycle oil on trouser leg
Hymns were hardly made to measure
Service strictly off-the-peg
Always worse when it's a young man
Wheezed an older woman's voice
Yes, I thought – a decent send off
Pay your money take your choice
Sleep forever in the graveyard
At the eastern edge of town
Toxic yew trees, raised umbrellas
English weather – pouring down

He'd been chef and I'd been porter
Fond of cricket kind to me
Strange the things that you remember
Liked a song by Kiki Dee
Working in a narrow kitchen
Deafened by the radio
Shouted jokes and muddled orders
Table five? Away you go.
Different blokes on different wages
Makes me sorry now I think
He was bringing up a family
I was spending mine on drink

He'd been ill – I got a phone call
Now I'm cycling in the rain
Wakes Colne White Colne
Earls Colne and Colne Engaine
Had to borrow shirt and jacket
He'd be laughing like a drain
Wakes Colne White Colne
Earls Colne and Colne Engaine

Nineteen miles from home to Halstead
Nineteen miles then back again
Had the notion that exertion
Might stave off potential pain
Coming home I passed a postman
And we spoke as cyclists will
Asked me was I in a hurry
Only to be living still

Past the Chappel viaduct
Only memories can remain
Wakes Colne White Colne
Earls Colne and Colne Engaine.

Under Milk Float . . . or Colchester Tales

In autumn – when fires are lit
I dream of broken fences in Cambridge Walk
Where conkers fall and spiky boys
Dog half-smoked spliffs en route to school

And by St Botolphs Circus
In Fagin's Den
I dream guitars and bullet-belted boys
And skinny girls who cry
In the amphetamine blue night

When the rain falls in Culver Street
The long-forgotten faces
From long-closed pubs
All asleep now walk beside me
Andy, Ted and Antoinette
Killed by drugs or motorbikes
Or coming home from parties
In the drunken dawn
All asleep now

In October – on Friday nights
I hear the hissing gas fires in Maldon Road
And the bedsit kids in thin black clothes
Who listen to The Mish – live on chips
Put their face on after work
Take their washing home to Mum
And spend all week in monochrome

On Scheregate steps I met the devil
Standing by the paper shop
Tired now and middle-aged
Smoking in a tracksuit top

In autumn, when the sky is slate
And Priory Street is misty
I dream the teenage soldiers
Kissing chubby schoolgirls
In Artillery Folley
One kiss for now
And one for the Shankhill Road

And Old King Cole
Can't claim the dole
They caught his fiddlers three
But he does alright
In the Middleborough night
With his black and white TV

In the High Street – by The Hippodrome
In the orange afternoon
I dream the oyster feast
The town council
The red carpet
For celebrities
To gorge themselves in the town hall
While some bag-lady
Goes down with reality poisoning
Outside Sloppy Joe's

In autumn – when fires are lit
I take a teatime bus up Greenstead Road
With rabid steamy shoppers in their android clothes
Who dream of Telecom vans
And double glazing
Of shopping as religion
And cable television

Of rain-splashed windows in Lexden Road
Of half-term lovers on Hilly Fields
Of half-heard sirens in Castle Park
Of swishing car tyres down Brook Street
And listen to me now
In Autumn – when fires are lit
I dream.

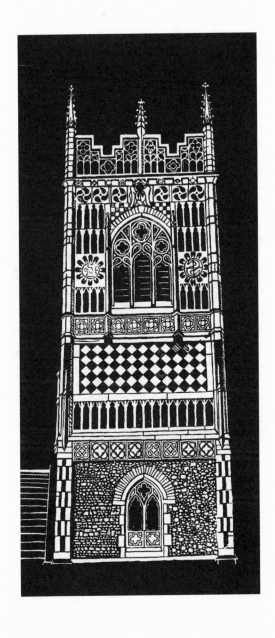

Dead in the Barmaid's Bed

Plywood coffin draped in sacks
Funeral feast of crisps and snacks
Poor man's Prozac – Special Brew
Massive turn-out, guests all knew
This is what the vicar said:
"Found him dead in the barmaid's bed"

Found him dead in the barmaid's bed
Lacy knickers on his head
What with all the gossip spread
Bound to raise his local cred

Women tutted, men said, "Odd.
There but for the grace of God.
Not behaviour I'd endorse . . . "
Envious as hell of course.
Seeing him in that state of grace
Hard to keep a serious face
Should have legged it. Died instead
Found him dead in the barmaid's bed

Man of Essex, thoroughbred.
Lead in pencil, gear in shed,
Brass in pocket, books in red,
Always kept his ferrets fed.
Found him dead in the barmaid's bed
Found him dead in the barmaid's bed
"Good owld buoy," they quietly said
Found him dead in the barmaid's bed.

Horses Seen Through Trees

Some silver autumn morning
Remember days like these
As horses seen through trees

And in forgotten orchards
The ochre of the sun
And echo of a gun

A gale bends the birches
The elders crick and groan
The moon is smashed to pieces
In waters of the Colne
And autumn drags you home

The dead are reacquainted
With living they have known
Their half-remembered faces
In flowers, moss and stone
Ashes, earth or bone

And if I die in early autumn
Light a fire boy – in the woods
Build it well and crack a bottle
Share out all my worldly goods

And on some silver morning
Remember days like these
As horses seen through trees.

They Also Surf . . .

Beach Boys tributes pour in from Essex

If Brian Wilson came from Clacton
And not the U.S.A.
He'd have a very different post code
From Californ-I-Ay
You'd find it hard to imagine
The way it might have been
Had everybody gone surfin'
CO17

Well East Coast girls are hip
I really dig those coats they wear
And the Southend girls
When they eat their chips
They knock me out when I'm down there
The Essex farmers' daughters
Wear their jodhpurs far too tight
And the Maldon girls
With the way they spit
At their boyfriends late at night
But I wish they all could be
Saffron Walden girls

Well she hasn't got a car
And you can't rely on Eastern Region
And the Frinton over-sixties surfers
Had a pretty poor season
And they're rather short of happening bands
At the British Legion
But she'll have Fun Fun Fun
Till her daddy takes the tea-bag away.

World of Chav

. . . Waynze a waangha see? Ah fahhghin'
Toldim we woz gaan dahn taahn
And like, we're in Blue-wor'a, righ'?
And we've go' all ar 'oods pulled daahn
We've gone t'tax this skyter-punk
Cos Daz'n'Nayfn's like . . . well-drunk
Righ'? This White Ligh'nin that they 'ad
S'wick-ed, man. S'like: "Ow bad?"
Aw mate! This skyter, anyway?
I smacked 'im. But the scur'ty guard?
S'come over. So e's got away
But e's like . . . naafin? Finkzees 'ard?
While Kev, yeah? E's got past the twat
An' nicked a Burb'ry bysebaw 'at,
I swopped him for a sovrin ring
I bough' yeah? Wiv some uvva bling

Tha's Chelsea, Jawwd'n and Danyella?
Wiv 'er bybee – sez it's mine
It ain't, righ'? It's that knob-ed Jay's
Ah int seen 'im abow' for days
S'workin' as a roofer naah
Juscoz they stopped his benefit?
Righ' Know'wo'mean? S'well unfair
K'ssaahndra's gunna bleach 'is 'air
Ah'd go out wiv 'er – well fit.
But Jay righ'? Sez she mings a bit.
Dahn Blue-wor'a ? Anyway –
I had this Nokia, in there, righ'?
Oi! You still got that dog a yors?
That brindle-poin'? Got wicked jaws
Faaghin' . . . seen it in a figh'.
Seez ya laters, yeah? O'righ'!

To Braintree –

Upon reading in a newspaper that its citizens
were the ugliest in Britain

To Braintree Essex, where I hear
The local population
Were this week nominated
As the ugliest in our nation
Where bride may turn the groom to stone
Who'd courage to unveil her
While groom departs for honeymoon
With pig-net and a trailer

Who slurs the name of Braintree
Rose of Essex, none serener?
The town is nice, the furry dice
In God's Own Ford Cortina.
We're honest here in Essex
If we've faults, then we admit 'em
But Braintree, ugliest? Not a chance . . .
No. That one goes to Witham.

Our New Love, The Bus

Let's take the 78 in early winter
When all the oaks are turning gold
From Tenpenny Hill to Thorrington
In mid-November sunlight after rain
And kiss outside the Co-op here
Till 4.16 . . . and then 4.36 . . .

THEN AT THESE MINUTES
    PAST EACH HOUR

Until the buses all stop running
A full hour short of closing time.
From now on sweetheart, it is only us
The driver and that gum-chewing girl
Who meets her mates at Brightlingsea
A shivering, knackered office cleaner,
An old bloke back from seeing a son in jail,
And some kid talking draw-deals on a phone.
For these will be our fellow travellers
The very young, the aged and the car-less

And out along the estuary at tea-time
The headlamps dash the fields and lanes
And rake the stops where no-one waits
Who ever graduated to a car

DO NOT STAND FORWARD
    OF THIS POINT

Past a pub, a sign, a level-crossing
The new estate lit up like Lucozade
Deserted, but for hooded boys on bikes
A bell, a groan of brakes, a hiss of doors
Then back onto the rabbit-splattered road
The rattling draughty taxi's now our own

So let us take this 78 in winter
While all the world is busy driving home
One to each car and cursing at the traffic
Because apart from us and all these ghosts,

34 SEATED AND NINE STANDING

We may well find, at last, that we're alone.

With Winter on the Woods

With winter on the woods these days
The east wind strafes the swings
Sheds its load in Bellevue Road
The cemetery sings
The hymns of sailors' sweethearts
For lovers run aground
From faded scripts upon the crypts
The ivy winds around.
The iron gates, the brickwork
The conker trees, the yew
The ghost of Captain Sainty
Still calling for his crew

With winter on the woods these days
She wears a widow's veil
Beautiful in middle age
If rather cruel and pale
And not a patch on summer, boys
Ah, that was an affair
Moved on.
I loved her.
Called her name
Too late – she wasn't there

The hawthorn cracks, the ditches fill
A grizzled wolf, I haunt that hill.
And hunger for the lime-gold spring
And watch young Adam, coppicing
But I won't cry, cos boys don't cry
Not even as the trains go by
Seen through a blue and smoky haze
The embers of remembered days

That memories are verdigris
Upon the soul, is all I know
And winter's on the woods again
And I return to Wivenhoe.

Jackdaws

The jackdaws on the chimney stacks await
While skeins of smoke from kindling in the grate
Go drifting over crisp and windless air
Towards the village roofs, remaining there
To hang like flimsy raiments on the square

The church, its railings, cupola and tower
The clock that never chimes the chilblained hour
But gazes over river, trees and streets
Remembering the souls that filled its seats
And how the pattern of the past repeats

Mysterious, laconic and profane
The jackdaws chack! and strafe the weather vane
Blue-eyed scaffolders, on shift all day
With squared-off neckerchiefs of silver-grey
They tell the world what weather's on the way

Watchful villains, staring slyly down
When winter fields have turned from green to brown
And sleep amnesic underneath the freeze
Where flecks of snow go floating on the breeze
An icing-sugar dust on days like these.

The Dark Days Down to Christmas

The dark days down to Christmas paw
Like horses at an earthen floor
When all the ghosts of autumn pass away
And ragged squads of starlings fight
In firethorn trees in fading light
For orange berries brighter than the day

The dark days down to Christmas slip
As convicts from a prison ship
Down moonlit ropes and hawsers, one by one
And past the quayside through the lanes
With winter dragging on their chains
Peer into windows, envious of the sun

The dark days down to Christmas creep
As wolves around a pen of sheep
When people turn their collars up and sigh
A convalescent crescent moon
Comes drifting out mid-afternoon
To bid an old arthritic year goodbye

And down the drain these dark days spin
As kindling wood and paraffin
And sacks of coal and logs are fed
Into a spider-haunted shed
The garden tools with cobweb tines
And skeins of string on withered vines
Are vestiges left hanging on
As evidence of summer gone

The dark days down to Christmas call
In echoes to a flagstoned hall
Too early for the feast, they stay awhile
But each, an uninvited guest
Is dirty, cold and under-dressed
And slips away unmissed, in single file

The dark days down to Christmas wait
Like cinders cricking in a grate
Before the fire is raked, re-set and lit
And cheerless in their unmade bed
Glow only very faintly red
But give no hint of heat in spite of it

And yet with each dark day complete
Lighter and brighter grows the street
As frantic in the pubs and shops
The work speeds up – for soon, it stops
And in a lull between the two
The last day, having much to do
Though up till now, no time for thought
Allows a warming glass of port

And having set an hour free
Before the lights go on for tea
As ingots of old sunlight pierce the gloom
A ghost parade of days appears
With paler days from other years
Who reminisce in whispers round the room

The last day down to Christmas ends
Excusing all his sullen friends
Who slave until December twenty-third
Cut mistletoe, deliver parcels
Light the cottages like castles
Scribble cards and hardly say a word

Then having done their tasks they drift
As workers from a graveyard shift
The moment that each day has lost its light
Till wistfully, the last one goes
Ignites a candle, leaves a rose
And slips out softly, to the frosty night.

Aldeburgh in January

Bitter sings the North Sea wind
That stabs through city clothes
And high the ragged herring gulls
Who screech
The leather-handed fishermen
Impervious to the cold
Will winch their boats up
On the shingle beach

The artist isn't drawing
The writer doesn't write
But walk in silence
Through the winter day
While in the frozen distance
The ghosts of ships long sunk
Tall-masted haunt their hopes
From far away

And all along the shoreline
The January tides
Come crashing through
The gateway of the year
To toast their unknown futures
In foam and muddy grey
A sea god flung a pint
Of dirty beer

Bitter still the North Sea wind
And better in the pub
The smell of seafood pies
And Suffolk ale
The cosy lunchtime murmur
And scrape of forks and knives
To drown the doubts of those
Who fear to fail.

List of Linocuts

The books: *Longshore Drift, The Shipwright's Trade, Peter Grimes, Wild Man of Orford*, and *Black Shuck* are available, amongst others, from Jardine Press Limited.